CHINESE
AIRLINES

CHINESE AIRLINES

Airline Colours of China

中國民用航空

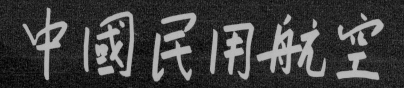

COLIN BALLANTINE
& PAMELA TANG

Airlife
England

ACKNOWLEDGEMENTS

The picture coverage for *Chinese Airlines* has taken fifteen years to collate, and gathering the research material has been even more frustrating despite China's open door policy since 1978. Still it's almost impossible to obtain official information about Chinese aviation history and get official permission to photograph civilian airliners.

Only your authors of *Chinese Airlines* know the immense difficulties we have experienced in presenting this book to the readers as accurately as possible.

Enormous efforts have been made to achieve the impossible and we are extremely grateful to the following people that have welcomed the idea of *Chinese Airlines* and made a co-operative effort to ensure the first ever book on Chinese airlines published in the Western world is accurate and successful: Beijing Capital International Airport, Foreign Affairs Department (Zhang Jianmin, Wang Yong, Kong Yue, Xin Qiang, Huang Wanyan); Ministry of National Defence, Foreign Affairs Bureau (Captain Zhao Bao, Colonel Gu, Lt Zhao PLAAF HQ, Lt Lu PLAAF HQ); Guangzhou-Baiyun International Airport, Foreign Affairs Department (Gary Yeh); China General Aviation Corporation, Taiyuan (Xia Yu Sheng, Vice-President, and his staff at Taiyuan-Wusu Airport); China Xinjiang Airlines, Urumqi (Zhang Rui Pu, President, and his friendly staff); China Flying Dragon General Aviation Company (Wu Cai Bao, general manager, Hua Jun Ping, vice-general manager, Cheng Jin Qong, vice-general manager, and all the helpful staff at Pingfang); Tianjin Municipal Administration of Civil Aviation, Foreign Affairs Department (Fan Rong Qiang and the staff at the CAAC Aeronautical College). China Northwest Airlines, Xian (Zhu Zhenyuan, director of Propaganda and Wang Wen Ming, chief of Promotions Department); China Southwest Airlines, Chengdu, Foreign Affairs Department (Guo Ning, Chong Gang Zhang, Huang Bo); Sichuan Airlines, Chengdu, Airline Planning (Liu Jia); China Southern Airlines, Guangzhou, Foreign Relations Division (Liang Jing Zhao, Director and Danney Liang); Mr Wu Ying Qi, Consular of Commerce and Trade, Perth, Western Australia; Tom Singfield of London-Gatwick and Hans Oehninger, Rolf Wallner, Marcel Walther all of Zürich-Kloten who came to the rescue at a late stage with a few missing pictures where credited. A final and special thank-you must go to Group Captain Bob Schroder, Chief Military Air Attaché and Warrant Officer Matt van der Lugt of the Australian Embassy, Beijing, both of whom played an important role in liaison with the various aviation authorities in China.

Copyright © 1995 by Colin Ballantine and Pamela Tang

First published in the UK in 1995
by Airlife Publishing Ltd

British Library Cataloguing in Publication Data
A catalogue record for this book
is available from the British Library

ISBN 1 85310 580 5

Printed in Hong Kong

Airlife Publishing Ltd

101 Longden Road, Shrewsbury SY3 9EB, England

Front Cover:
Of the seven Yak-42s operated by China General, only two, *B-2754* and *B-2756*, are painted in the full airline colours. The one-hundred-and-twenty-seat airliners operate from their Taiyuan base to Beijing, Changsha, Chengdu, Fuzhou, Guangzhou, Haikou, Hangzhou, Nanjing, Sanya, Shanghai, Shenzhen, Wenzhou and Xiamen. *B-2754*, operating the daily flight GP7303, shines in the morning sun as it approaches Guangzhou airport in November 1993.

Rear Cover:
B-2930 and *B-2931* parked up at Urumqi in May 1994. Two Boeing 737-300s were delivered to China Xinjiang in December 1993 and January 1994 for use on the main tourist air routes of China.

Title Page:
A look into the passenger past of China General. The airline operated seven magnificent Il-14s, three Russian-built and four Czechoslovakian Avia 14s from 1976 until their retirement in 1993, when their routes were taken over by the Y-7-100s and Yak-42s. Only *623* and *625* were lucky enough to be painted in China General's attractive red and blue colours for their inter-provincial routes. In a rare action photograph, *623* is seen lifting off for a one-hour flight to Xian.

Previous Pages:
On a warm and sunny afternoon in 1993, Sichuan Airlines Tu-154M, *B-2624* waits on the taxiway for its turn to take-off from Guangzhou's single runway. Regrettably this area is now fenced off and no longer can one spend an enjoyable day photographing aircraft from the Baiyun Road, Guanzhou.

INTRODUCTION
CIVIL AVIATION IN MODERN CHINA

Mystery and intrigue have always been associated with aviation in China for the past seventy years. After some serious research during many visits to China, we are able to present this concise history of events in the Chinese aviation industry and airlines.

In March 1919, the Ministry of Communications of the Chinese Government (the Northern Warlords) set up an office to establish civil aviation in China. Immediately eight British-built Vickers Vimy aircraft were purchased from the United States of America to operate passenger services within China. Foreign pilots were recruited not only to fly the aircraft, but to train the Chinese pilots. A route network was established from Beijing to Shanghai, Guangzhou, Chengdu, Harbin and Kulun (now known as Ulan Bator, the capital of Mongolia). These planned routes were never implemented except for two part legs of two routes, from Beijing to Tainjin commencing in May 1920 and Beijing to Jinan commencing the following year. Beijing to Tianjin operated for one year and Beijing to Jinan survived only ten days. A small number of temporary flights were operated from Beijing to Beidaihe as well as some tourist flights over the Great Wall of China during the summer days. These early pioneering flights were all suspended by 1924 pending a restructuring of civil air operations.

During the latter part of 1923 a new aviation proposal was passed by the Chinese Government to authorise the then famous American-Chinese pilot and manufacturing engineer Mr Yang Xian Yi to purchase aircraft and spare parts. Together with Mr Chen Zhuo Lin, Mr Lin Wei Cheng and Mr Nie Kai, who were trained in the United States, he came back to Guangzhou to establish a new civil aviation industry in China. Appointed by Dr Sun Yat-Sen, Mr Yang Xian Yi became the general director of the Civil Aviation Bureau and head of Guangzhou Aircraft Manufacturing Factory. The following year, in 1924, under the leadership of Dr Sun Yat-Sen, an aviation college was set up at Guangzhou. During the first two years of 1925 and 1926, the college trained 527 pilots who contributed a great deal to the development of Chinese aviation, and some even lost their lives to it.

The Chinese Government was ready with the newly restructured civil aviation system and by 1929 had purchased four American-built Stinson Reliant aircraft and recruited two foreign pilots and one foreign mechanic, supported by three Chinese pilots and nine mechanics. The Shanghai to Nanjing route started in July 1929. Unfortunately the route was irregular; however, it did manage to survive just over a year and during that time carried a total of 1,477 passengers and twenty kilograms of mail.

The air services were again suspended until August 1930, when the Chinese and American Governments founded a joint venture Sino-American company named CNAC–China National Aviation Corporation; the Chinese held fifty-five per cent of the shares and the Americans held the remaining forty-five per cent. CNAC initially operated the five-seater Stinson SM68 airliner from Beijing, Shanghai, Guangzhou, Chengdu and Chongqing to fourteen other destinations.

In February 1931, a second joint venture company was formed between the Governments of China and Germany; the Chinese held seventy-five per cent of the shares and the Germans held the remaining twenty-five per cent. The outcome of this venture was Eurasia Airlines, operating six-seater Junkers W33 airliners across Asia into China. However, from the beginning it was beset with problems and after a few months of operations the venture decided to base the fleet of two Junkers F13s, six Junkers W33s, six Junkers W34s – and later, into the 1930s, nine Junkers Ju52s and one Junkers Ju160 – in China serving an intense network of routes in the south-eastern corner of China.

The American Government, in April 1933, transferred its shares to Pan American Airways. CNAC then took delivery of two new eight-seater Douglas Dolphin flying boats and six Douglas DC-2s. Later, in 1937, two Consolidated Commodore flying boats and several Douglas DC-3 Dakotas joined the fleet.

The Chinese Government had at last found a successful solution to building a stable civil aviation structure despite the Japanese invasion of Manchuria. In aviation attention was drawn away from north-east China when in June 1933 the local government of Guangdong and Guangxi set up Southwest Airlines with three airliners. Local domestic routes were flown and the company's only international route operated from Guangzhou to Hanoi via Zhanjiang. By July 1937 the airline had ceased operating.

The Japanese invasion of China had by August 1937 taken a serious turn for the worse with the Japanese attacks penetrating deep into mainland China. In August 1937 CNAC and Eurasia moved their base from Shanghai to Hankou and Xian due to the movements of the invading Japanese. In January 1938, the headquarters of CNAC moved from Hankou to Chongqing and the maintenance base moved to Hong Kong. Later the same year, in October, the base of Eurasia was again moved from Xian to Kunming.

Part of China was occupied by the Japanese whilst other parts were controlled by the Kuomintang led by Chiang Kai Shek. In 1938 the Kuomintang and the Communists formed an alliance that was to be the birth of Soviet involvement in China; hence a Sino-Soviet airline soon followed. The Chinese Ministry of Communications and Aeroflot of the Soviet Union signed an agreement in September 1939 to provide air services between Hami in the far north-western corner of Xinjiang Province and Alma Ata. The airline was simply known as Hamiata.

By 1939, China was again in turmoil with the Japanese invasion of their country and the start of World War II which was beginning to spread east from Europe. The first aviation casualty was Eurasia, caused by the breaking of diplomatic relations between China and Germany; the German share of twenty-five per cent was taken over by the

Chinese Ministry of Communications which declared Eurasia to be a Chinese State-owned airline. The airline then fell into more trouble as a direct result of the continuing Japanese occupation. The fleet of airliners was based in Hong Kong and had been severely damaged by Japanese bombing, all except one Junkers Ju52. Eurasia held its last board of directors meeting in February 1943 at Chongqing.

Meanwhile, China's other airline, CNAC, was making history. The airline became the first in the world to lose an airliner when a DC-2 was shot at by a Japanese fighter. The airliner somehow managed to land but was strafed on the ground killing all fourteen occupants. The airliner was salvaged and rebuilt only to suffer the same fate again two years later in October 1940.

CNAC built its history and reputation on courage and determination when in April 1942 it began flying supplies on the famous India–China Hump route. CNAC bore the brunt of the burden of flying this incredibly difficult and dangerous route over some of the worst mountain terrain in the world. Back-up arrived in April 1943 in the shape of the United States 10th Air Force. Amazingly, CNAC lost only one DC-3 and that was on take-off at Kunming during the airlift to India.

Central Air Transport Corporation (CATC) was formed from the remnants of Eurasia in March 1943. Mr Chen Zhuo Lin was appointed as general manager of CATC which gratefully accepted eleven old passenger transport aircraft from the Chinese Government. Both CATC and CNAC continued to provide limited air services until the Japanese were finally driven out of China in August 1945. Progress in Chinese aviation became rapid with CATC buying five C-47s and three C-46s from the United States Air Force in November 1945. CATC were still expanding, and between April and July of 1946, twelve C-47s and three C-46s arrived, again from the United States Air Force. In 1947 another five C-47s arrived and by August 1949 the airline had taken delivery of six Convair CV-240s, amounting to a total fleet of forty-two airliners.

From January 1949 to the end of 1952 considerable upheaval occurred in Chinese civil aviation. The first major event in January 1949 was the moving of the headquarters of CATC and CNAC to Taiwan, Hong Kong and Guangzhou, and by the middle of the year both airlines operated ninety-nine airliners comprising C-46s, C-47s, C-54s and the six Convair 240s. The next major event was the founding of the People's Republic of China on the first day of October 1949. This milestone in Chinese history changed the face of the Chinese aviation industry.

November 1949 proved to be a turbulent month for Chinese civil aviation. On the second day of the month the Chinese Government decided to establish CAAC – Civil Aviation Administration of China – under the People's Military Committee which appointed Zhong Chi Bing as the first general director of CAAC. On the ninth day of November 1949, only five weeks after the foundation day, the employees of both CATC and CNAC, led by their general managers Mr Chen Zhou Lin and Mr Liu Jing Yi, were directly involved in an unusual company uprising in Hong Kong when a formation of twelve airliners filled to capacity with employees fled the island of Hong Kong to be repatriated with their motherland, rather than be exiled in Hong Kong. The aerial convoy was led by Convair 240 *XT-610* and eagerly pursued by three C-46s and eight C-47s. Regrettably, on that fateful day in November, the twelve escapees left behind seven deliberately destroyed aircraft on the ground and the remaining seventy C-46s and C-47s were impounded, their fate unknown. Both airlines had seventeen other airliners on the mainland and, together with the repatriated twelve, the total of twenty-nine airliners became the foundation for the formation of the CAAC fleet. After this historic announcement CATC again moved its base and headquarters to Guangzhou, and CNAC did likewise to Tianjin.

Into the new decade of 1950, the People's Central Government of China named the leading aircraft of the repatriation flight from Hong Kong: the Convair 240 *XT-610* was officially named *Beijing* and Chairman Mao Tse-tung gave his personal inscription to this aircraft. During the early months of 1950, CAAC set up aviation stations on existing aerodromes in Tianjin, Guangzhou, Chongqing, Kunming and Lanzhou and soon commenced passenger charter flights from Beijing to these new stations.

The Chinese and Soviet Governments held many official high-level discussions on joint venture routes and aircraft supply. All the plans and meetings held during the previous year became reality when on the first day of July 1950 the first schedule international service of the new Sino-Soviet airline was flown from Beijing to Chita, Irkutsk and Alma Ata. The Sino-Soviet partnership commenced domestic routes on the first day of August 1950 when two routes were inaugurated, one being Tianjin–Beijing–Hankou– Guangzhou–Chongqing, the second Chongqing–Chengdu–Guiyang–Kunming using borrowed Aeroflot Li-2s and Il-12s. During the latter half of 1950, the first batch of the CAAC Li-2s was delivered allowing CAAC to develop more domestic routes.

In the spring of 1951, swarms of flies and mosquitos needed urgent extermination because of widespread damage to the sub-tropical areas around Guangzhou in southern China. CAAC called on the general aviation division to modify a Curtiss C-46 Commando as an insect sprayer. Many sorties were flown until the C-46 had successfully completed its task. At that time the C-46 was by far the largest aircraft in China ever to be used as an insect sprayer. The next task awaiting the C-46s was in July 1951 when three C-46s flew a total of 120,000 kilograms of food and general supplies in fifty flights over Tibet, most of which were dropped from the air in mountainous terrain.

CAAC, still without an airline image, formed CPAC – China People's Aviation Company – as an airline from its base at Tianjin in July 1952. The fleet of forty-five aircraft, comprising mainly C-46s and C-47s complete with CPAC titles, opened thirteen new routes, ten domestic and three international. The airline was short-lived and ceased operations in December 1952. After six months' flying, a total of 200,000 passengers was carried and 2,047 tons of cargo and mail.

The Civil Aviation Administration of China then used its initials of CAAC as its airline name and identity. 1952 also saw the introduction of four Ilyushin Il-12 airliners with CAAC. Ten Czechoslovakian-built Aero 45s were purchased from the Soviet Union in 1953 for aerial mineral exploration and geological and forest surveying. The Aero 45s were retired during 1960 in favour of Yunshuji Y-5s and Lisunov Li-2s.

The following year, 1954, the four-year joint venture Sino-Soviet airline came to an end with China buying out the Soviet fifty per cent share. However, China continued to buy large quantities of Russian-built aircraft for its expansion plans into the 1960s. The versatile Antonov An-2 biplane was ordered by CAAC and the first examples arrived in 1955 for passenger and general aviation use. The same year the famous repatriation Convair 240 named *Beijing* was selected to fly the proving flight Beijing–Chengdu–Lhasa (the capital of Tibet).

During 1956, the first of many Ilyushin Il-14s were flown from the Soviet Union to take up their new positions with CAAC. The following year many Czechoslovakian-built Avia 14s and East German-built VEB 14s joined the fleet to make CAAC a very large operator of the Il-14. CAAC published official figures in 1957 revealing that a fleet of one hundred and eighteen aircraft comprising Aero 45s, An-2s, Il-12s, Il-14s and Li-2s, all of which had replaced the remaining C-46s and C-47s. The only Western-built airliner flying in China between 1957 and 1963 was *Beijing,* the Convair 240.

In May 1958, CAAC opened the new international route from Beijing to Ulan Bator, Mongolia using the new Il-14s. The new route allowed Mongolian Airlines to use their Il-14s from 1960 to 1966 to Beijing. Meanwhile, in December 1958, CAAC dispatched a Li-2 to Vietnam to photograph and survey the vast forest areas of central and southern Vietnam.

As passenger demand for flying grew within China a larger type of airliner was required. CAAC evaluated and chose the turboprop Ilyushin Il-18 fitted with one hundred seats. During 1959 the first of twelve examples arrived in Beijing, giving excellent service for the next thirty years. Internationally, the CAAC Il-18s carried the Chinese flag to new territories previously out of reach for China. Il-18 *208* operated the first VIP charter carrying Guo Mo Ro, the famous Chinese archaeologist, poet and vice-chairman of the Standing Committee for the China National People's Congress, to Indonesia. This flight was the first time a Chinese airliner was chartered to fly over a vast area of sea.

With the large amounts of Soviet-built airliners operating in China, CAAC made a surprise move by buying five British-built Vickers Viscounts in 1963 for domestic routes.

During June 1965, Il-18 *208* was again making history by carrying Premier Zhou En-lai on a fourteen-country State visit to central Africa, the first time a CAAC airliner had visited the African continent. The following month Il-18 *212* carried Deng Xiao Ping to Romania on a State visit, this being the first time CAAC operated a VIP charter to Europe.

CAAC continued for the next six years to open more domestic routes and to improve the infrastructure of the corporation. During this six-year period many new bilateral airline agreements were signed allowing CAAC greater access to countries wishing to do trade with China. The turning point for CAAC came in 1971 when the first of five jet airliners arrived from the Soviet Union. The four-engined Ilyushin Il-62s were able to operate intercontinental routes to Moscow and eastern Europe, and of course cut the Il-18's flying time by half with a superior range.

From the early 1970s, China's economy became stronger and this enormous country with its enormous population started to become a major trading nation that required many aircraft for travel, modernisation and expansion. Between 1973 and 1984, CAAC ordered over two hundred aircraft from Western and Russian manufacturers: first came the Boeing 707, followed by the British Trident, the Soviet An-24, Boeing 747SP, Boeing 747-200 and Boeing 737.

China's elder statesman and architect of modern China, Deng Xiao Ping, stated in one of his speeches in 1980 that civil aviation must adopt the road of enterprise. His motivating words were followed by an important policy reconstruction by CAAC. The same year, CASC – China Aviation Supply Corporation – was established, responsible for the purchase of aircraft, engines, spare parts, maintenance equipment and a considerable amount of ground handling equipment required for China's many airports. It took a further four years of planning for CAAC's next historic move in Chinese aviation, when in 1984 CAAC transformed its massive aircraft fleet into eight major airlines to operate under their own identity. Gradually the airliners proudly appeared in their new identity overseen by CAAC.

From this historic date in 1984, the Chinese airlines continued their expansion with the following types appearing in China: A-300 and A-310 Airbuses, BAe-146s, Beechcraft Super King Air, Boeing 747-400s, 757s and 767s, Canadair Challengers, Cessna Citations, De Havilland Twin Otters and Dash-8s, Fokker 100s, Gates Lear Jets, Ilyushin Il-76s and Il-86s, Lockheed L-100-30 Hercules, McDonnell Douglas MD-80s and MD-11s, Pilatus BN-2 Islanders, Piper Cheyennes, SAAB 340s, Short 360s, Tupolev Tu-154Ms, Yakovlev Yak-42s and helicopters from Russia, America, England and France. This influx of modern aircraft has now put Chinese aviation firmly on the map as a respected buyer and operator, securing China's aviation future for many years.

Since the early years of the twentieth century, China's aviation has flown through many turbulent times. Fortunately, their history has been preserved as part of the national heritage collection from the 1909 Feng RU-2 biplane to the Ilyushin Il-62 four-engined jet airliner. This historic and priceless collection of over two hundred aircraft can be seen on public display at the Datang Shan Aviation Museum, Changping, near Beijing, which provides an insight into the glorious past of China's aviation history.

Civil Aviation Administration
of China (CAAC)

This very rare Douglas DC-3 aircraft was one of the original China National Aviation Corporation 'Daks' that flew the World War II supply route, the famous China Hump airlift. The aircraft survived until the formation of CAAC in 1949 and operated many flights until its retirement around 1956. The aircraft then disappeared into storage to an unknown location as part of China's aviation heritage. *XT-115* then re-appeared as an exhibit when the Datang Shan Aviation Museum at Changping opened in November 1989.

(Left)
The only surviving Convair 240 from the original fleet of six. The actual aircraft, *XT-610*, was the only Convair 240 to return to the Chinese mainland after the employees uprising in Hong Kong during October 1949. The following year *XT-610* was named *Beijing* by the People's Central Government, and Chairman Mao Tse-tung wrote the Beijing titles for this special aircraft. *XT-610* was then chosen to operate the official inaugural CAAC flight from Guangzhou–Baiyun airport in August 1950; it was then repainted in CAAC colours and registered as *401*. Unfortunately this fine example at the Datang Shan Aviation Museum at Changping is without engines and propellers.

(Below)
Convair 240, number *401*, was the sole example of this type operated by CAAC. The airliner was incorporated into CAAC from Central Air Transport Corporation in 1949 and had the distinction of being the first CAAC airliner to bear the CAAC titles personally designed and written by Premier Zhou En-lai. *401* is believed to have operated until the early 1970s when it was withdrawn from use and parked at Beijing Capital airport for many years. Sometime around 1985–1987, the airliner was moved to another airfield where it was repainted in its original colours of CATC – Central Air Transport Corporation – and subsequently moved to the Datang Shan Aviation Museum at Changping for display as part of China's national aviation history.

In 1950, CAAC ordered their first Soviet-built airliner, the twenty-one seat Lisunov Li-2. Thirty airliners were ordered to operate CAAC services to every corner of China, and they also played an important role in general aviation as aerial photographic aircraft. The Li-2 survived for twenty-two years as a passenger carrier until the type was retired in 1972. Most of the fleet was then passed to various Government aviation groups who used the Li-2 as pilot trainers, calibration aircraft and aerial surveyor and general purpose freighters, mainly from CAAC's general aviation headquarters at Taiyuan. The Li-2s in this role survived until 1982 when they were finally retired after giving thirty-two years of solid reliable service. *315* is seen in her last days before retirement at Taiyuan. As far as our research indicates, only two complete examples have survived, although a few fuselages can still be found at various airports. *305* now resides at the CAAC Aeronautical Instructional base at Tianjin and *311* is preserved and displayed at the Datang Shan Museum at Changping together with five other excellent examples from the Chinese Air Force.

(Above)
Four Ilyushin Il-12s were purchased by CAAC in 1952 to supplement the Li-2s. Unfortunately their history with CAAC is virtually unknown; one civil example exists at the CAAC Aeronautical Instructional base at Tianjin. The Chinese Air Force operated at least twenty-four Il-12s and two examples in good condition are displayed at the Datang Shan Aviation Museum at Changping.

(Left).
Every country that has a purchase agreement for aircraft with the Soviet Union operates the magnificent Antonov An-2 radial-engined biplane. A few early examples of the Soviet-built version flew in China during the 1950s. Since the early 1960s, China has manufactured the An-2 under licence as the Shijiazhuang Yunshuji Y-5. The first production line was established at Nanchang, Jiangxi Province, followed by the second line at Shijianzhuang, Hebei Province. During its thirty-year Chinese production approximately five hundred have been built to 1992. Most are still active as crop sprayers with the general aviation divisions of the newly-formed airlines; most other roles performed by the Y-5 have been taken over by the Chinese-built Y-12.

In 1956, the need for more airliners in China became evident as passenger demand grew. Between 1956 and 1960, fifty-two Ilyushin Il-14s were delivered to CAAC not only to supplement the overworked Li-2s but to service CAAC's new routes to their neighbouring countries. The Il-14s became the backbone of the propeller fleet for many years, and when eventually retired from service many found a new life with fledgling airlines after CAAC had disposed of them. *628*, a Soviet-built version, awaits its next flight from Guangzhou in 1982.

(Left)
Many Il-14s were finished in bare aluminium, as was *621*. This airliner was built in Czechoslovakia as an Avia 14 and delivered to CAAC in May 1959. Thirty-four years later in 1993, *621* was retired and awaits its fate at Taiyuan. Good photographic results were not expected at Taiyuan in November 1993 owing to heavy rain that continued overnight. The next morning when the rain stopped for an hour or so, the results were spectacular.

(Below)
Fifteen Mil Mi-4 helicopters were purchased by CAAC in the mid-1950s for industrial, survey, aerial construction and fire fighting. These interesting-looking and robust, piston-engined helicopters were rarely seen at the provincial airports in China during their twenty-year stay with CAAC. The fleet of fifteen when retired was passed to the military with the exception of *713*, as illustrated, which went to the CAAC Aeronautical base at Tianjin as an instructional airframe helicopter. The Chinese aviation industry built many Mi-4s under licence for the Chinese Air Force, designated the Z-5. Two military examples, both in excellent condition, are displayed at the Datang Shan Museum at Changping.

In 1958, the Government of the Soviet Union under President Nikita Khrushchev presented *678* to the Chinese Government as a gift for VIP use. Premier Zhou En-lai received the airliner and used *678* on many occasions to travel within China and to neighbouring countries. Visiting Heads of State President Sukarno of Indonesia and President Ho Chi Minh of Indo-China (now Vietnam) were amongst a number of dignitaries who flew in *678* in its heyday. The airliner was passed to CAAC during the mid-1960s as a normal passenger transport and survived until its withdrawal in 1993. *678* is seen here at Taiyuan, Shanxi Province awaiting removal to a museum.

(Above)
The Ilyushin Il-18 was the first turbo-prop airliner operated by CAAC and with its superior range took over many Il-14 international routes and high density domestic routes. Thirteen Il-18s were operated by CAAC spanning thirty years. An additional three examples were leased from Tarom between 1985 and 1988 to cover the early withdrawals of the older Il-18s. *212* is seen on a schedule service to Rangoon in 1973 still bearing its original roof fin and the old numbering system.

(Left)
B-208 in later years was used as a normal passenger version for CAAC and is seen here at Beijing in 1985. These handsome airliners were retired in 1989 and replaced by the Boeing 737 jetliners. Two examples, one from CAAC and one from China United Airlines, are preserved at the Datang Shan Museum at Changping. *B-210* is the third known survivor at the CAAC Aeronautical Instructional base at Tianjin.

In a surprise move by CAAC, the Government ordered five Vickers Viscount turboprop airliners that were also the last five Viscounts ever built. They operated on CAAC domestic routes from 1964 to 1982 until replaced by Boeing 737s. Four were sold in the Philippines and one remained in service with China United Airlines. *B-404* is seen at Hong Kong on one of its many visits for routine maintenance.

(Left)
It is estimated that forty-two An-24s were delivered to CAAC to meet the increased passenger demand on China's domestic routes. The first An-24 arrived in 1969 and the last one was delivered in 1974. *B-428* in its original condition moves towards the runway at Guangzhou-Baiyun airport in October 1980 for its next flight back into the interior of China.

(Below)
In 1984 the entire An-24 fleet was re-registered with their four-figure system and allocated to the various regional carriers. *B-3402* still retains its CAAC colours, but it is operated by China Northern Airlines and is seen at Beijing Capital airport in June 1987. Most of the An-24s are still active into 1995; however, many are scheduled to be replaced with the Chinese-built Yunshuji Y-7 turboprop airliner which is virtually an identical airliner.

(Above)
The age of jet airliners arrived at CAAC with the first of five Ilyushin Il-62s in 1972 for use on the CAAC routes to Moscow and Bucharest via Karachi. The first CAAC Il-62 in its original form was sighted in the West at London–Heathrow airport in June 1973. The airliner flew an aviation delegation to London to finalise the purchase of the de Havilland Trident airliners. *2024* flew for CAAC for fourteen years until 1986 when it was retired. It now resides at the Datang Shan Museum, Changping as the largest airliner on display.

(Right)
B-2022 was the first CAAC Il-62 to be delivered in December 1971 and soon became the regular Il-62 on the Moscow route. *B-2022* also visited London in January 1977 again in connection with the Trident purchase. The airliner is seen here at Beijing Capital airport in 1987 passing the familiar rows of pine trees that line the taxiway opposite the main terminal building. Regrettably all airliners eventually come to the end of their useful life and, during 1993, *B-2022* was dismantled for scrap together with *B-2020*, *B-2026* and *B-2028*.

Thirty-eight An-26s are known to have operated in China as domestic freighters for Government agencies. *787* is seen here at Taiyuan operating a flight for China United Airlines.

The British-built de Havilland Trident tri-jet was purchased in 1973 as part of an enormous modernisation plan to improve domestic services with emphasis on comfort, reliability and speed, and to replace many ageing Soviet-built propeller-driven airliners. Initially CAAC bought four Trident Mk 1s from Pakistan followed by thirty-three Trident Mk 2Es and two Trident Mk 3s direct from England. The Trident Mk 2Es operated two international routes to Hong Kong and Ulan Bator, Mongolia, and domestically the Tridents could be found at Beijing, Shanghai and Guangzhou and at most of the provincial capitals' airports throughout China. *B-248*, a Trident Mk 2E, is seen here at Beijing Capital airport in its original form.

(Above)
After 1984, the entire Trident fleet was re-registered with the four-figure sequence as seen on *B-2203*. Ten Trident Mk 2Es and both Trident Mk 3s were transferred from CAAC to China United Airlines for military and government use. The last CAAC Tridents were withdrawn during November 1991 after operating their last schedule flight from Harbin to Beijing in October 1991. The CUA Tridents continued until June 1992 when they were replaced by the new CUA Boeing 737s.

(Left)
Only two of the lengthened Trident Mk 3s were operated by CAAC. Once these two examples left the Hatfield factory they were rarely seen operating in China. They were passed to China United Airlines during 1984 for military use. The picture shows *G-BAJM*, the last Trident Mk 3 built, awaiting delivery at Hatfield to be flown to China to become *B-270*. *(Tom Singfield)*

In 1966, CAAC took delivery of a small number of Antonov An-12 freighters for domestic cargo use. The aircraft with their twenty-ton capacity played an important role in transporting heavy components into the industrial areas of China whilst industries were being upgraded during the 1970s. The An-12s have spent most of their lives based at Taiyuan and Tianjin and were passed to China General Aviation Corporation in 1984. *B-201* (later to become *B-3151*) is seen in its original form undergoing routine maintenance at Beijing Capital Airport.

B-3151, alias *B-201*, flew for China General Aviation Corporation from 1984 to 1992 in full CAAC colours as illustrated. The aircraft was laid up during 1992 at Tianjin and has not moved since.

The Mil Mi-8 helicopter first appeared in China in 1972 when the first of nineteen were delivered. Their role was to replace the ageing Mi-4s and to support the expansion in the oil industry in southern China. Several Mi-8s were allocated to the CAAC Shenyang Regional Administration, which based them at its helicopter branch at Changchun airport in Jilin Province to fight the destructive pine forest fires that frequently occur in that area. The Mi-8 can dump two tons of water from its tanks on to a fire. Later in 1979, when more Western-built helicopters were purchased, the Mi-8s were moved north to work with CAAC industrial division. Five years later in 1984, ten Mi-8s were transferred to China General Aviation Corporation and the remaining nine moved to China Northern Airlines, general aviation division.

(Left)
After the initial success of the Trident as regards its reliability and image, CAAC then invested in the Boeing 707 intercontinental jet to develop new air routes to the United States of America and Europe. The Boeing 707 was also used as a flagship for the Chinese Government on Heads of State and trade delegation flights to Western countries. The fleet of Boeing 707s were delivered as 'combi' aircraft with a large port side forward cargo door. Later in life, three examples were converted to pure freighters. In 1984, with the transformation of CAAC, the Boeing 707s were passed to Air China, China Southwest Airlines and Shanghai Airlines. *B-2414* is seen standing at London–Gatwick airport operating a passenger flight back to Beijing. *(Tom Singfield)*

CAAC soon saw an enormous economical difference between the Il-62 and the Boeing 707 with the American jet being far more reliable and considerably easier to maintain, and most importantly it afforded easy access to the Western idea of interchangeable and compatible spare parts. CAAC then signed a multi-million dollar agreement with the Boeing Aircraft Company to supply a wide range of jet airliners to take Chinese aviation well into the 1990s. First to arrive was the Boeing 747SP to replace the overworked Boeing 707s on the San Francisco route in 1980. Like the Boeing 707, the 747SP was easy to maintain and economical to operate. The four examples were passed to Air China in 1984. *B-2454* is pictured at London–Gatwick airport. *(Tom Singfield)*

(Right)
During 1981, three Antonov An-30 aerial survey aircraft were bought by CAAC to replace the ageing Li-2s and Il-14s. The three aircraft were originally based at Beijing with CAAC's industrial division, then later moved to Taiyuan. In 1984, all three aircraft were renumbered and passed to China General Aviation Corporation still retaining their original CAAC markings. The An-30 as an aerial survey aircraft works as a low- to medium-height camera ship. Currently only one An-30 is still employed as a camera ship operated by China General Aviation Corporation in CAAC colours.

(Below)
B-3303, originally one of the three camera ships, now operates a different role after its transfer from CAAC to China General Aviation Corporation. Together with *B-3302*, the aircraft, still in CAAC colours, flies the frequent mail runs from Guangzhou to Dalian. *B-3303* awaits minor maintenance at Taiyuan-Wusu airport on a very wet day in November 1993.

Towards the end of 1982, the first of over one hundred Boeing 737s arrived in China. Their purpose was to provide passenger comfort and encourage tourism between the main tourist centres. The early Boeing 737s were the -200 series later followed by the -300 series, both of which had enormous passenger appeal for CAAC. *B-2509* is seen on the taxiway awaiting departure at Guangzhou in the late afternoon sun.

(Left)
B-2512, another CAAC Boeing 737-200, is seen here approaching Guangzhou on short finals early one morning.

(Left)
1983 saw CAAC take delivery of the world's biggest jet airliner, the Boeing 747-200 series. The airliners were employed on the long haul eastbound route Beijing-San Francisco and the long haul westbound route Beijing-Zürich and Beijing-London. After the arrival of the Boeing 747, the smaller Boeing 707s were rarely seen in the Western world and the Ilyushin Il-62s were relegated to routes within China. *B-2450* is seen here after pushback at Zürich-Kloten Airport ready to return to Beijing. *(Hans Oehninger)*

(Above)
The next Western-built airliner to appear in the familiar CAAC colours was the Airbus Industrie's A-300 and A-310. The A-300 series was used on high density routes within China mainly from Beijing, Shanghai and Guangzhou. The A-310s spent most of their time on routes to Hong Kong, Osaka and Karachi.

With continued passenger demand and the need for more wide-bodied containerised airliners, the Boeing 767-200 was the next airliner to arrive in CAAC colours. Initially, the Boeing 767s were used on the Hong Kong route and later, as more of the extended range Boeing 767-300s were delivered, they operated as far as Moscow, Stockholm, Vienna and Sharjah. The same year, in 1985, the first of several Boeing 757 narrow-bodied airliners also arrived in CAAC colours. *B-2551,* a Boeing 767-200 is seen departing from Guangzhou-Baiyun Airport operating a domestic flight to Beijing.

(Left)
The CAAC industrial division needed a medium- to high-altitude aircraft for their aerial survey work. Three Beechcraft Super King Airs were introduced in 1986. Two examples, *B-3551* and *B-3552* were used for aerial survey work and later transferred to China General Aviation Corporation at Taiyuan. The third aircraft, *B-3553* was retained by CAAC as a calibration aircraft and based at Beijing Capital Airport.

(Below)
B-2707 is one of four BAe-146 jet airliners transferred from CAAC to Air China. One aircraft based in Hohhot operates both international services from Hohhot to Ulan Bator, Mongolia and Chita in Eastern Siberia and the sole domestic service to Hailar, Manchuria, close to the Russian border. The three remaining BAe-146s operate domestic schedules from Beijing and Hohhot to the regional capital cities and tourist destinations with a high level of serviceability. *B-2707* is seen approaching Guangzhou in November 1993.

(Right)
CAAC in 1982 agreed with McDonnell Douglas to buy five DC-9-82s, otherwise known as the MD-82, for use on high density routes mainly from Shanghai in the east and Shenyang in the north-east. *B-2132* in full CAAC colours is seen here on short finals at Beijing Capital airport.

(Below)
CAAC MD-82 prepares for take-off from Guangzhou's Baiyun airport.

In the south of China the 1980s oil boom was in full swing. Helicopters and the oil industry are two of a kind and it became necessary that the Sikorsky S-76 join the CAAC industrial division for oil industry support. The S-76s are based at Zhuhai.

The British-built Shorts 360 was selected
by CAAC as a short-range inter-provincial
feeder airliner. Eight examples were
delivered in 1985 configured as thirty-seat
airliners. The fleet, although in CAAC
colours, quickly transferred to the China
Eastern and China Southern Airlines.
B-3605 stands in the Guangzhou sun
during June 1987.

The first commercially operated Yunshuji
Y-7 turboprop airliners were delivered to
CAAC in 1984 for evaluation but did not
enter service until 1985. Since this date
the entire basic version Y-7s – fifteen
airliners were built – have all been
delivered to CAAC in their colours and
operated as such by most of China's larger
airlines. *B-3454*, a basic forty-eight-seat
version, waits at Beijing Capital airport for
its next turn of duty in June 1987.

In 1986, after CAAC took delivery of their first locally-manufactured airliner, another Chinese-built aircraft, the Yunshuji Y-12, was delivered to CAAC. The turboprop general purpose aircraft was purchased to supplement and eventually replace the piston-engined Yunshuji Y-11. Most of the Y-12s were destined for the general aviation divisions of the CAAC Regional Authorities and have retained their original CAAC identity until 1991, when China Flying Dragon were the first Y-12 operator in China to use their own titles. *B-3815*, in full CAAC colours, is one of five operated by China General Aviation Corporation from its base at Changzhi.

(Left)
As relations with the Soviet Union improved during the mid-1980s, both Governments discussed airliner requirements. China was offered the low cost Tu-154M resulting in a steady flow of deliveries since 1985. Currently thirty Tu-154Ms have been delivered to CAAC for distribution to the four principal operators who have applied their own colours.

(Below)
CAAC also took delivery of the Tu-154M for Government use. All Tu-154M airliners in the *B-4xxx* series are operated by the Government fleet; however, most of the airliners carry China United Airlines titles. Pictured here at Nanyuan Air Force base is a newly delivered Tu-154M, *B-4027*, with CAAC titling registered to China United Airlines.

(Right)
In January 1992, CAAC received the first of six Yakovlev Yak-42, 120-seat tri-jet airliners. The fleet of airliners was immediately passed to China General for passenger route expansion. *B-2751* waits in the late afternoon Guangzhou sun for departure to Taiyuan.

(Below)
B-2751, again at Guangzhou, is seen inbound from Taiyuan.

Air China (CA)

Air China International Corporation was the first airline in China to be made independent from the giant CAAC's First Fleet. Air China is also the major international carrier for China operating direct flights to Europe, Africa, America, Australasia and the Middle East. The international division operates from Beijing Capital airport, and next to the original Beijing terminal building is the maintenance area capable of maintaining and servicing their large Boeing fleet. The domestic headquarters are based at Hohhot in the autonomous province of Inner Mongolia, north-west of Beijing. The division operates and maintains the Yunshuji Y-7s and the fleet of BAe-146s.

The latest addition to the Air China fleet and currently the flag carrier of the airline is the Boeing 747-400 operating the high density routes to Tokyo and Osaka and the long haul routes to Frankfurt and Paris. *B-2464* awaits its next turn of duty at Beijing Capital airport.

CAAC transferred the ownership to Air
China of the four Boeing 747-200 combis
currently operating to Sharjah, Rome and
New York via Anchorage. The four combis
have been the backbone of Chinese air
freight exports for several years until the
delivery of the Boeing 747-200 freighter.
B-2446 is seen parked at Beijing Capital
airport on a cold Sunday afternoon in
November 1993 awaiting its next duty the
following day.

(Left)
B-2462 was originally the last Boeing 747-200 combi to be delivered in 1987. Two years later it was dispatched to the United States for conversion to a pure freighter with a carrying capacity of 105,000 kilograms. The aircraft returned in 1990 to take up its position on schedule cargo flights to Frankfurt, Moscow and New York. *B-2462* is seen at Beijing Capital airport in the summer of 1991.

(Below)
Air China's fleet of ten Boeing 767s took over the routes of the ageing Boeing 707s between 1985 and 1987. The four Boeing 767-300s operate the longer range flights to Moscow, Vienna, Dubai, Cairo, Karachi and Kuwait whilst the Boeing 767-200s cover the shorter routes to Tokyo, Fukuoka, Singapore, Jakarta and Bangkok. *B-2557*, a Boeing 767-300, rests at Beijing Capital airport awaiting the start of another week's flying.

(Right)
B-767-300, *B-2557* approaches Guanzhou-Baiyun Airport inbound from Beijing operating flight CA1321.

(Below)
The Lockheed L-100-30 Hercules, of which CAAC purchased two examples in December 1987, spent two years in CAAC colours although operated by Air China Cargo, the freighting division of China General Aviation Corporation. Both aircraft were based and maintained at Taiyuan; however, they spent most of their time operating from Fuzhou to Nagoya exporting live eels. Three years later in 1990, both L-100s were repainted in China Eastern Cargo colours under a joint venture between China Eastern and China General. A further two years on in 1992, both L-100s were transferred to Air China Cargo together with the sole An-12 freighter and based at Tianjin. Illustrated is *B-3004* at Tianjin in immaculate condition in June 1993.

All ten Boeing 707s were passed from CAAC to Air China in 1985 to retain their passenger services. As more Boeing 767s were delivered, some Boeing 707s became surplus to requirements. With China's increase in air cargo exports, *B-2414* was converted to a pure freighter in the colours of Air China Cargo. Another surplus example went to Shanghai Airlines, four went to China Southwest Airlines and Air China retained four examples for charters, although these have subsequently been retired. The Air China Boeing 707 freighter still operates cargo schedules from Tianjin and Shenzhen to Singapore. *B-2414* is seen here at Beijing Capital airport operating as a passenger airliner before its conversion to a freighter.

Air China currently operates eighteen Boeing 737-300 series. The only international routes using the Boeing 737 are from Beijing to Ulan Bator, Mongolia and Rangoon, Myanmar (formerly Burma). The remainder of the fleet operate domestic routes mainly from Beijing to the provincial Chinese cities and tourist destinations. *B-2535*, a Boeing 737-300, waits on the end of the taxiway in preparation for take-off from Guangzhou bound for Baotou.

Seen on final approach at Guangzhou; Boeing 737-300 *B-2581* inbound from Shijiazhuang.

CAAC continued its connection with the British aircraft industry when in 1986 they ordered fifteen BAe-146 airliners. The early examples took over the Trident route to Ulan Bator, Mongolia and later served the smaller regional towns in the northern half of China. *B-2707* waits at Beijing Capital airport for its next duty to Ulan Bator.

(Left)
Up to 1992, the Air China Yunshuji Y-7s were regular visitors to Beijing; however, with the purchase of more jet airlines, the fleet of six now operates within Inner Mongolia to the towns of Chifen, Tongliao, Ulanhot and Xilinhot. The only Y-7 route outside of Inner Mongolia is to Shijiazhuang in Hebei Province. Air China currently operates three basic Y-7s and three Y-7-100s with the vertical winglets. Here one of the basic models, *B-3463*, shares the apron with a bicycle.

(Below)
The two China General Aviation Corporation An-12s, both in CAAC colours, were transferred to Air China Cargo during 1992. *B-3152* was sent to Russia for a complete rebuild. The aircraft returned from Russia in full Air China Cargo colours to operate alongside the two L-100-30s. *B-3152* resides on the ramp at Tianjin in May 1994, a few months after returning from Russia.

(Above)
The general aviation division of Air China operates a large number of Yunshuji Y-5s and Y-12s from several bases in Inner Mongolia. One such unique example is Y-5, *B-8032* complete with logo and titles. The aircraft is fully fitted with spray bars for agricultural work. A further local modification is seen on the top wing tip. The three stabilizers provide a smooth turn without losing height during crop dusting. This rare example was parked at Tianjin in June 1993. Behind this aircraft is Trident *B-2207* in good condition.

(Right)
Air China operates six of the older Boeing 767-200s with a distinctively shorter fuselage. *B-2556* awaits its passengers on Gate 1 at Xian-Xianyang Airport for a return flight to Beijing in March 1995.

China Southern Airlines (CZ)

China Southern Airlines was established in 1986 based on the previous Guangzhou Regional Administration as one of the big eight airlines in China, and is easily identified by its distinctive blue tail flower logo; its headquarters is in Guangzhou. The airline operates sixty-seven Boeing airliners, twenty-two turboprop airliners, eight helicopters and twenty-one Yunshuji Y-5s for crop spraying. With a total of one hundred and eighteen aircraft China Southern Airlines is by far the largest Chinese airline. In 1992 China Southern, operating one hundred and sixty-two air routes, surpassed all previous records and carried 8.04 million passengers to become the number one airline in China for that year.

The Zhuhai heliport is the China Southern helicopter base housing two Dauphines, four S-76As and two Bell 214s. The helicopters are employed under contract to maintain services to the offshore petroleum industry. Also based at Zhuhai are the BN-2 Islanders used for short haul charter flights between Guangzhou, Zhuhai, Shenzhen and the island of Sanzao where the new Zhuhai airport has recently been completed. The China Southern Airlines general aviation division operates eighteen Yunshuji from Hengyang, Shashi and Nanyang. The fleet is mainly engaged in crop spraying and aerial surveying.

The Boeing 767-300ER is the largest airliner in the China Southern fleet with six examples. The airliner operates the international route from Guangzhou to Singapore and Bangkok. Domestically, the airliner operates to Beijing, Shanghai and Hangzhou. *B-2562*, previously operated by Malev of Hungary, awaits departure from Guangzhou.

B-2564 is seen here on final approach to
Guangzhou.

(Above)
Nineteen Boeing 757s are operated by China Southern and all are powered by Rolls-Royce RB-211 engines. The Boeing 757 fleet is configured as a 200-seat airliner comprising eight first class seats and one hundred and ninety-two economy seats. Four Asian destinations are serviced by the Boeing 757: Kuala Lumpur, Singapore, Bangkok and Jakarta. *B-2806* moves off the taxiway and prepares to turn on to the runway at Guangzhou in November 1993.

(Left)
The China Southern Boeing 757s operate from Guangzhou to all the provincial cities throughout China, to Urumqi in the far north-west and Harbin in the far north-east. On final approach to Guangzhou is the first Boeing 757 to be operated in China. *B-2801*, still looking like new, has been with China Southern since September 1987.

(Right)
China Southern fly the Boeing 737 internationally to Bangkok, Hanoi, Manila and Vientiane. All other Boeing 737 routes are within China. A total of forty-two Boeing 737s carry the China Southern colours comprising seven of the older -200 series with the long thin Pratt & Whitney engines, and the remaining thirty-five are all -300 series. *B-2515*, a -200 series, is seen here approaching Guangzhou.

(Below)
B-2525 is one of the many 140-seat Boeing 737-300s operated by China Southern. The airliner waits on the taxiway for runway clearance at Guangzhou.

(Above)
B-2921 gleams in the late afternoon sun at Guangzhou in November 1993. This aircraft is one of two China Southern 737 "QC" (quick change) combi's and at the time of photographing was only two months old.

(Left)
N999CZ is the only Boeing 737 in the China Southern fleet to carry a foreign registration, being leased from C.ITOH Leasing. The airliner awaits departure from Guangzhou.

(Above)
Four Swedish-built SAAB 340 turboprop airliners based at Shenzhen operate the China Southern routes to Beihai, Guangzhou, Hengyang, Nanning, Ganzhou, Sanya and Zhanjiang. *B-3652* prepares for take-off from Guangzhou to Shenzhen.

(Right)
SAAB 340 *B-3653* on final approach to Guangzhou.

Three Shorts 360 turboprop airliners were transferred from CAAC to China Southern. Originally the Shorts 360s were used as a feeder airliner from provincial cities and towns in the south-east region of China to Shanghai. With the increasing number of modern jetliners in this region, the Shorts 360s now operate from their Wuhan base to Enshi, Shashi, Changzhou, Nanjiang and Huangshan. *B-3608* awaits its next turn of duty at Shanghai in February 1993.
(Rolf Wallner)

(Left)
During 1989, China Southern took delivery of five Pilatus Britten-Norman BN-2 Islanders. The five aircraft are used for passenger and small freight services from their base at Zhuhai to Guangzhou, Sanzao and Shenzhen. *B-3901* is seen approaching Guangzhou.

(Below)
China Southern operated five Antonov An-24s until recently replaced by five Yunshuj Y-7s. The fleet is now based at Zhengzhou and operate local inter-provincial routes to Nanyan, Xian, Wuhan, Yichang, Hefei, Taiyuan, Guilin, Shashi and Huangshan. During March 1995, *B-3456* is leaving the afternoon sun at Xian-Xianyang Airport operating flight CZ372 bound for Nanyang.

China Eastern Airlines (MU)

China Eastern Airlines, formerly the CAAC Shanghai Regional Authority, was established in December 1987 from its existing base and headquarters at Shanghai–Hongqiao airport. The secondary base, catering for domestic services only, is situated at Nanchang and the general aviation division is housed at Hefei. China Eastern control eighty aircraft from the Yunshuji Y-5 to the latest high-tech MD-11. By the end of 1995, China Eastern will have taken delivery of their first four-engined A-340 Airbus, of which five examples are on order.

China Eastern, up to 1993, operated four A-300-600 Airbuses. Demand was so high that in 1994 a further six examples joined the fleet for the expansion of services to Tokyo, Osaka, Nagoya, Fukuoka, Singapore, Bangkok and Seoul. The A-300s also operated within China to Beijing and Guangzhou. *B-2308*, inbound from Shanghai, approaches Guangzhou.

In May 1991, the first of six MD-11s was delivered to China Eastern for their long haul international services eastbound through Japan to Los Angeles and Seattle, and westbound to Bahrain and Brussels. Five months later in October 1991, the sole MD-11 freighter arrived to take up its role supporting Shanghai's export manufacturers flying their products to Seattle, Chicago, Bahrain and Brussels. A further four MD-11s configured as forty-six first class and two hundred and ninety-four economy seats were delivered to meet the demand of tourism and the constant flow of business personnel supporting Shanghai's industry. China Eastern Airlines have a maintenance contract with Swissair for major overhauls on MD-11s and A-300/A310 Airbuses. *B-2171* is seen at Zürich-Kloten Airport on one such visit to the MD-11 facility.

(Hans Oehninger)

(Above)
Thirteen MD-82 airliners fly the China Eastern colours around the provincial cities of China. The MD-82 also operates two international routes to Hong Kong and Seoul. *B-2135* prepares to land at Guangzhou in November 1993, after a flight from Hefei.

(Left)
The two China Eastern A-310s are confined to the three times weekly Shanghai to Nagoya flight and occasionally are used for back up to the larger A-300 Airbuses. *B-2305* is seen at Zürich-Kloten Airport after a visit to the maintenance area. Photographed in superb light conditions, after a rain-storm, by Hans Oehninger.

The only Fokker 100s in China are flown by China Eastern. Ten examples are based at Nanchang and operate internationally to Nagasaki and Hong Kong and domestically to Guangzhou, Kunming, Shanghai and Shenzhen. *B-2236* approaches Guangzhou inbound from Nanchang.

(Left)
The Yunshuji Y-7, of which China Eastern operate ten examples, provides air services from Hefei and Nanchang to Fuzhou, Ganzhou, Hangzhou, Huangshan, Ningbo, Wenzhou and Wuhan. The Y-7s are rarely seen at Shanghai as they have been forced into inter-provincial routes since the mass introduction of jet airliners. *B-3453* is seen here at Beijing Capital airport in October 1990, before the turboprop airliner ban at Beijing.

(Below)
Three BAe-146s originally with CAAC were transferred to China Eastern in 1988. The three examples were operated by the airline's secondary base at Nanchang on feeder services to Shanghai and rarely seen anywhere else. During 1993 all three aircraft were withdrawn from use and stored pending the sale back to British Aerospace. This happened during November 1994. *B-2705* is seen at Shanghai in May 1989.

China Southwest Airlines (SZ)

China Southwest Airlines was founded in October 1987, formerly known as the CAAC-Chengdu Regional Administration. The airline operates its entire jet airliner fleet from the Sichuan Province capital of Chengdu-Shuangliu Airport utilising twenty Boeing 737-300s, twelve Boeing 757s, five Tu-154Ms and a sole Boeing 707 freighter. The jet fleet operate three international routes from Chengdu to Kathmandu, Bangkok and Singapore using Boeing 757s and daily schedule charter flights to Hong Kong using the Boeing 737. The airline's domestic network serves forty-six Chinese cities covering a total route length of 160,000 kilometres. The general aviation division of China Southwest Airlines is based at Chongqing-Jianbei Airport in the eastern part of Sichuan Province. Chongqing is responsible for all Yunshuji Y-7 flight operations where three examples serve local and neighbouring provincial towns and cities. The airline also operates from Chongqing four Yunshuji Y-12s; one example is a general purpose freighter and the remaining three are fitted as crop sprayers. The sole China Southwest Boeing 707 is operated by the general aviation division and based at Chengdu. Since 1987, China Southwest has established many of its own facilities at Chengdu-Shuangliu Airport some of which include in-flight catering and a cargo warehouse. The achievements peaked in May 1994, when a new maintenance hangar was commissioned capable of holding two Boeing 737s and one Boeing 757 under complete cover. The airline has an attractive red, white and blue colour scheme with a blue logo centralised on the tail representing the winged head of an eagle that resides in the mountainous regions of Sichuan Province.

China Southwest operates twelve Boeing 757s. Two of the routes are international, one being Chengdu–Singapore, and the other can only be described as the rooftop route of the world from Lhasa, the capital of the mountainous region of Tibet, to Kathmandu, Nepal, high in the Himalayan range. *B-2821* prepares to land at Guangzhou in November 1993.

(Above)
The Boeing 757s of China Southwest fly to all the major cities and provincial capitals and tourist routes in China. *B-2820* awaits its turn for take-off from Beijing.

(Left)
Seventeen Boeing 737-300s are currently operated by China Southwest. *B-2522* wears the original titling of the airline now superseded by new titles in Chinese and English. The airliner is awaiting loading at Beijing Capital airport in June 1992.

(Right)
B-2534 is one of several Boeing 737s that operate schedule charters from Chengdu to Hong Kong and Bangkok, Chongqing to Hong Kong, and Guiyang to Hong Kong. The airliner is approaching Guangzhou for landing in November 1993.

(Below)
Eight Yunshuji Y-7s operate local air services with Sichuan Province mostly to Chongqing. *B-3479* was used by China Southwest Airlines in a joint route sharing agreement with Wuhan Airlines from Chengdu to Wuhan. The only airliner used is seen during its brief career with both airlines in November 1993, carrying full China Southwest colours and titles and the Wuhan Airlines logo on the tail.

(Above)
The faithful and reliable Boeing 707 has been operated by the Chengdu Regional Authority of CAAC for many years. The four original aircraft – *B-2408*, *B-2410*, *B-2412* and *B-2418* – were the first airliners of China Southwest to wear the new red colours. Into 1995, the Boeing 707 fleet has been reduced to one aircraft. *B-2412* and *B-2418* have been sold to the U.S.A. *B-2408* awaits its fate at Chengdu and the sole survivor is *B-2410* operating as a pure freighter. *B-2410* is fitted with a roller-bed floor throughout and capable of carrying thirteen PIP contoured pallets. This aircraft operates four flights per week at night to Guangzhou and two flights per week during the day to Xiamen. The picture shows *B-2410* in combi configuration at Beijing Capital Airport operating a passenger service before Boeing 757s took control of the Chengdu-Beijing route.

(Left)
Five Tu-154Ms are on hand to support the air routes from Chengdu to Beijing, Guangzhou, Shanghai, Nanning, Guilin, Ningbo, Shenzhen, Dalian and Urumqi. *B-2616* is seen here on final approach to Guangzhou in November 1993.

China Northwest Airlines (WH)

China Northwest Airlines was the last of the eight principal airlines to be formed from CAAC in December 1989 and based on the structure of the former Northwest Civil Aviation Division. The airline operates from the ancient and historic city of Xian (formerly known as Changan) and capital of Shaanxi Province which is also the original starting point of the famous "Silk Road" route through to the Middle East. Throughout the 1980s air traffic was steadily increasing into the tourist destination of Xian and the original airport of Xian-Xiguan was unable to cope with the expansion. A new airport was built some fifty kilometres from Xian City and is known as Xian-Xianyang Airport that became the new operating base for China Northwest Airlines. A modern maintenance facility was also built to service the fleet of airliners currently comprising five A-300 and three A-310 Airbuses, nine Tu-154Ms and seven BAe-146-300s. The airline has a second fully equipped maintenance base at Lanzhou, north of Xian in Gansu province and home of the airline's general aviation division who operate three BAe-146-100s, six Yunshuji Y-7s on local and inter-provincial routes. Several Yunshuji Y-5 and Y-12 aircraft are reserved for agriculture and survey work. The first five years have been a successful and progressive development period for China Northwest who started with forty-eight inherited air routes from CAAC and by 1995 has grown to eighty-five air routes. The network radiates from Xian and Lanzhou to over fifty cities in China and internationally to Hong Kong, Nagoya with Singapore and Tashkent to be operated by the end of 1995. The logo of China Northwest Airlines is two horizontal half worlds separated by the Feitian Goddess.

Three A-310 Airbuses fly for China Northwest from their Xian-Xianyang base operating services to Beijing, Shanghai, Guangzhou, Harbin and Shenzhen. The airliners are rarely seen outside of China. *B-2301* awaits its next turn of duty at Xian-Xianyang in the early morning sun during March 1995.

(Above)
Five A-300-600 Airbuses are operated by China Northwest as the principal airliners of the fleet of thirty-seven airliners. The Airbuses serve the main cities of Beijing, Shanghai and Guangzhou and on occasions visit Hong Kong on tourist charters.

(Left)
The BAe-146 has been the mainstay of China Northwest since the airline's founding in 1989. The airliners operate on all the regional services and most of the provincial routes. The three BAe146-100s are based and operated from Lanzhou whilst the BAe146-300s operate from Xian-Xianyang. *B-2717* is parked at Xian-Xianyang waiting to operate flight WH2555 to Hangzhou in March 1995.

(Above)
China Northwest Airlines operates the second largest fleet ot Tu-154Ms in China. The nine airliners serve most of the provincial cities of China. *B-2620* is seen at Guangzhou, inbound from Xian operating WH2329 during November 1993.

(Right)
Provincial and local services of China Northwest are provided by a fleet of seven Yunshuji Y-7 turboprop airliners. Based at Xian-Xianyang, the Y-7s operate to Chengdu, Chongqing, Hanzhong, Huangshan, Wuhan, Yanan, Yinchuan and Yulin. Ad-hoc flights are also operated from Lanzhou. *B-3445* takes a rest at Xian-Xianyang whilst the crew take lunch during crew training for the day in March 1995.

China Northern Airlines (CJ)

China Northern Airlines from the north-east corner of China was founded in 1988. The airline's headquarters and base at Shenyang–Taoxian airport is the capital of Liaoning Province and shares its provincial borders with the Yellow Sea and North Korea. The province is an industrial region rather than a tourist area. The airline's secondary base further north at Changchun is the capital city of Jilin Province. The airline operates only four types: the A-300-600 Airbus, the MD-82, the Yunshuji Y-7 and the Mi-8 helicopter. The eleven Yunshuji Y-7s operate the local inter-provincial routes from Changchun and Shenyang. The general aviation division operates nine Mi-8 helicopters mainly on industrial and aerial construction work.

China Northern Airlines are the largest operator in China of the McDonnell Douglas MD-82. China Northern use the airliner on four international routes to Pyongyang, Khabarovsk, Irkutsk and Hong Kong. Domestically the MD-82 can be found at most of the airports of the principal cities and provincial capitals of China. *B-2104* is approaching Guangzhou inbound and non-stop from Harbin. All MD-82s in China operate with a 145-seat interior.

(Above)
China Northern leased two A-300 Airbuses in May 1993 from AWAS. Their performance was successful enough to warrant the purchase of another six examples for their long-haul, high density routes within China. *B-2312* is preparing for take-off for Beijing Capital Airport during September 1994. *(Marcel Walther)*

(Right)
China Northern Airlines operate eighteen MD-82s built by SAIC-Shanghai Aircraft Industry Corporation. One such example is *B-2136* awaiting its passengers at Xian-Xianyang on its return flight to Dalian on a sunny Sunday afternoon during March 1995.

China General Aviation Corporation (GP)

Formed from the Second Fleet of CAAC in 1987, China General Aviation Corporation, formerly known as China Industrial Aviation Service Corporation, specialise in aerial photography and remote sensing, with a small passenger transport capability. The company had five branch bases prior to 1992 with its headquarters at Taiyuan-Wusu Airport in Shanxi province. Also in 1992 one of its branches, China Air Cargo was transferred to Air China Tianjin branch with its four freighters; two L-100-30 Hercules and two Antonov An-12s.

The company has two helicopter bases at Tianjin and Handan.

The Bell 212s operate from Tianjin and the MBB-105s and Mi-8s operate from Handan, where previously the company's Lama and Alouette IIIs were housed. These two helicopter branches, together with another CGAC base at Changzhi airport, are engaged in general aviation operations, onshore and offshore petroleum service, aerial photography and filming, mineral exploration, agriculture and forest survey and spraying.

The passenger transport branch based at Taiyuan is a growing force, previously operating Il-14s as passenger airliners; the airline now operates three Yunshuji Y-7-100s and five Yakovlev Yak-42s.

B-2754 prepares for take-off from Guangzhou airport bound for Taiyuan in November 1993.

(Right)
Three Yunshuji Y-7-100s operate China General's routes from Taiyuan to Beijing, Chengdu, Chongqing, Shenyang, Tianjin, Wuhan, Xian and Zhengzhou. *B-3473*, at Beijing Capital airport in October 1990, wears the short-lived blue colours of the airline before the red and blue colours were adopted.

(Below)
B-3481 rests at Taiyuan-Wusu Airport in the afternoon sun during May 1993.

(Above)
The three CGAC Y-7s provide inter-provincial services for the airline and are still the only airline company in China permitted to use a Y-7 on schedule flights into Beijing. *B-3473* is seen moving off blocks at Xian-Xianyang operating flight GP7404 to Taiyuan.

(Left)
Nine Bell 212 helicopters, most of which are based at Tianjin, are used to support China's oil industry, especially the Bohai Sea oilfield, a gulf region north of the Yellow Sea. The fleet of helicopters is employed on a wide variety of duties from ferrying workers to and from the rigs to aerial maintenance of the towering platforms, and they provide a constant source of supply for the rigs. *B-7704* is parked at Tianjin between duties in May 1993.

Two of China General's Mi-8 helicopters are contracted to operate tourist flights over the incredible Great Wall of China. The helicopters fly this scenic tour from Changping heliport in Changping County approximately fifty kilometres north-west of Beijing. *B-7809* is returning from one such flight and preparing to land at Changping in June 1993.

Xinjiang Airlines (XO)

China Xinjiang Airlines was founded in 1985 from the former CAAC Xinjiang Regional Authority whose base was and still is Urumqi–Diwobao airport. The region shares its international borders with Mongolia, Russia and India, and due to its geographical remoteness relies heavily on air transport. The airline operates three Il-86 Airbuses, six Tu-154Ms (two of which are leased from Aeroflot), three An-24s and two DHC-6 Twin Otters.

During the latter half of 1993, China Xinjiang took delivery of three new Ilyushin Il-86 Airbuses for the routes eastbound to Beijing and westbound to Moscow. *B-2018* is parked up on a quiet Sunday morning in May 1994 at Urumqi.

(Above)
B-2019 parked up awaiting its next flight to Beijing.

(Right)
Tails of the Il-86s.

Tu-154M *B-2611* moves across the taxiway framed by the giant Il-86.

(Right)
B-2621 gleams in the early morning sun as it stands outside the main terminal building. The script on the roof of the building typifies the ethnic community mix in this interesting part of the world. The translated name is Urumqi, on the left is normal Chinese script, and on the right is Uigur script which is the local ethnic language.

(Below)
A lovely line-up of China Xinjiang Tu-154Ms at Urumqi. Two other Aeroflot Tu-154Ms are leased by China Xinjiang in normal Aeroflot colours.

China Xinjiang operate three Antonov An-24s – *B-3421*, *B-3425* and *B-3428* – for their routes from Urumqi to Asku, Altay and Yining. *B-3428* prepares to leave the ramp at Urumqi operating flight XO9915 to Asku on Sunday morning, 29 May 1993. Asku is close to the Kazakhstan border on the edge of the Taklimakan Desert.

China Xinjiang operate to the remote townships of Fuyun, Karamay, Korla, Kuqa and Qiemo with two DHC-6 Twin Otters. These aircraft are ideal for the short rough landing strips in this remote and inhospitable region of the world. *B-3505*, operating flight XO9931, prepares to leave the ramp at Urumqi for the eighty-five minute flight to Korla. On arrival at Korla, *B-3505* will take on more fuel during its thirty-five minute stop. The versatile DHC-6 will then continue for another sixty-five minutes to Kuqa, a town on the Silk Road just north of the Tarim Basin. The area of Kuqa is home to thousands of Buddhist caves and four ancient ruined cities, all of which are of historical importance dating back thousands of years. Well worth a flight on the DHC-6.

(Above)
Two Boeing 737-300s were delivered to China Xinjiang in December 1993 and January 1994 for use on the main tourist air routes of China. *B-2930*, awaiting passengers, is being prepared to operate flight XO9509 to Xian and Jinan on Sunday, 29 May 1994.

(Left)
The old and the new. In China the airport authorities operate some classic vintage service vehicles. At Urumqi–Diwobao airport the China Xinjiang engineering staff use this Chinese-built left hand drive motorbike and sidecar. In defiance of the age difference it roars away from the new Boeing 737-300.

81

China United Airlines

The Chinese Air Force has for many years provided a large number of transport aircraft for troops, officers, Government and military officials. Two years after the CAAC restructuring in 1986, the passenger division of the Chinese Air Force was formed as China United Airlines. The Air Force base at Nanyuan was used as the headquarters and base airport with a secondary base at Foshan near Guangzhou. Many vintage Il-12, Il-14 and Li-2 airliners in military markings were used until 1986, when the airline retired these types and slowly restocked with CAAC cast-offs, namely the Tridents, and purchased a small number of new airliners such as the early Tu-154Ms. By 1988 the VIP Boeing 737-300s had arrived together with the VIP Canadair Challengers. As the airline grew, its old military identity was gradually replaced with a more civilianised image, and into 1995 China United is now a profit-making, self-sufficient Chinese airline, but still holding the lucrative military contracts for air transport throughout China.

The sole Vickers Viscount was the first airliner to appear in full CUA colours. Fortunately, upon its retirement in 1989, *50258* was dispatched to the Datang Shan Museum at Changping for display as part of the national aviation collection, as seen here in February 1992.

(Above)
Seven Ilyushin Il-18s are believed to have been operated by China United, all of which were transferred from the Air Force. Only two are known to have survived and both are parked out of service at Nanyuan. *50851* even with its faded paintwork still looks elegant in the sun at Nanyuan in May 1994.

(Left)
China United operates fourteen Antonov An-24s and at least four Yunshuji Y-7s. Most of the fleet are based at Nanyuan. *51051*, a 1973 model RV with a tail loading ramp, was with the Chinese Air Force since new and was transferred to China United in 1986. The aircraft is seen on a sunny day at Nanyuan in May 1994.

(Right)
Front end of An-24 CUA-*51050* at Nanyuan.

(Below)
Several CAAC An-26 freighters were transferred to China United during 1991 for civilian contract work. One such example, *785*, is parked at Taiyuan in October 1993.

The China United Tu-154Ms were purchased as replacements for the ageing Tridents. The first four Tu-154Ms of China United were the first Tu-154Ms to fly in China, and currently the airline operates fifteen examples from Nanyuan. *B-4001*, the first Tu-154M to be delivered in China, arrived in Nanyuan in June 1985 and is seen on the Nanyuan flight line on a wet Monday in November 1993.

(Right)
In September 1992, China United bought three surplus and relatively new Tu-154Ms from Czechoslovak Airlines. The three examples are distinguished by their red CUA tails and are based at Nanyuan.

(Below)
During mid-1991, China United took delivery of three Ilyushin Il-76MD freighters. The aircraft have been used outside of China in support of the United Nations work in Cambodia. Within China, their forty-ton capacity has proved useful with heavy industry manufacturers in transporting generators and the like into remote developing areas of China.

China Flying Dragon Airlines

China Flying Dragon Aviation Company, using the airline name of Feilong Airlines, was founded in 1985 as the commercial division of Harbin Aircraft Manufacturing Company. Flying Dragon do not operate scheduled passenger services; however, certain aircraft are used for specialised passenger charters. The company's main function is agricultural and forestry work and both types of surveying, industrial and protection over land and sea. The Flying Dragon base is situated at Pingfang, some seventy kilometres north-east of Harbin City in a very remote rural area of Heilongjiang Province that shares its international border with the Russian Far East Federation. The company operate the DHC-6 Twin Otter, Yunshuji Y-12 and Y-11 for general aviation duties, and the Aérospatiale Ecureuil helicopter for forest fire fighting and protection.

Four DHC-6 Twin Otters, previously with CAAC, now proudly display the Flying Dragon colours. All four aircraft are basically 'quick change' from nineteen seats to a freighter or a specialised surveyor. *B-3502*, fitted as a survey aircraft with its cockpit bubble observation window, is seen at Pingfang in May 1994.

(Above)
B-3804, a Yunshuji Y-12 Mk II, is a specialised surveyor fitted with a tail probe for remote sensing. Owned and operated by Flying Dragon, it is one of many Y-11s and Y-12s seen at Pingfang in May 1994.

(Right)
Most of the Flying Dragon's piston-engined Y-11s are being retired in favour of the turboprop Y-12s. One of the few remaining Y-11s still active at Pingfang is *B-3882* bearing its China Flying Dragon titles and CAAC nose logo.

Flying Dragon operates eight French-built Aérospatiale Ecureuil helicopters for the Ministry of Forestry. The fleet of helicopters are used for forest surveillance, and surprisingly in this cold region of north-east China forest fires are a summer problem, therefore the fleet are fitted with hooks for attaching fire buckets to fight the fires. *B-7424* is parked at Pingfang.

(Above)
China Flying Dragon is under contract to supply services to CMS–China Maritime Survey. This interesting Y-12 Mk II is the sole example; fortunately *B-3807* was on the ground being prepared for another flight. The aircraft carries a sensor tube under the fuselage for the detection of fish shoals and is also fitted with sensor equipment to monitor the level of pollution in the Yellow Sea between China and Korea. The four Chinese characters on each side of the fuselage read China Maritime Survey.

(Right)
B-3807 carries this smart logo design on both sides of the nose. The top line in Chinese script reads China National Oceanic Administration.

China Xinhua Airlines

China Xinhua Airlines was established in August 1992 and commenced flying operations in June 1993. The airline was formed in Beijing as a municipal airline under a joint venture between the Beijing Municipal Government and the financiers of the airline. The name Xinhua means New (Xin), China (Hua) – New China Airlines. The airline operates five Boeing 737-300s from their Beijing base and two secondary bases at Tianjin and Shenzhen to Changzhou, Haikou, Hefei, Jinan, Kunming, Qingdao, Shanghai, Shenyang, Wenzhou and Xian.

Boeing 737-300 *B-2908* is parked at Tianjin in June 1993 awaiting delivery to China Xinhau.

Shanghai Airlines

Shanghai Airlines is the oldest and largest of the municipal airlines in China, originally established in 1985 by the Shanghai Municipal Government. For the first three years of operations the airline used the Boeing 707 and Boeing 757 airliners in the colours of CAAC until their own identity was established in the form of an attractive red colour scheme. The airline does not fly internationally, within China the familiar red colours of Shanghai Airlines can be seen in most provincial capitals and cities.

The original flag-carriers of the Shanghai Airlines fleet were two Boeing 707s. *B-2425* awaits its return flight to Shanghai from Beijing during May 1989. This was the only Boeing 707 to eventually receive the full Shanghai Airlines colours.

Shanghai Airlines Boeing 757 *B-2808* eases on to the end of Guangzhou's runway for take-off to Chongqing, operating flight SF386.

In the mid-morning sun at Guangzhou,
Boeing 757 *B-2833* makes a fine sight as it
approaches inbound from Shanghai.

Xiamen Airlines

During the spring of 1991, the Municipal Government of Xiamen formed Xiamen Airlines to operate air services from their base at Xiamen-Gaoqi International airport. The airline has one international route being a daily service to Hong Kong, all other routes serve Beijing, Shanghai and Guangzhou and all provincial capitals and tourist destinations. The airline has grown steadily from its single Boeing 737-200, *B-2524*, to operate seven Boeing 737s and three Boeing 757s from its base located at Xiamen on the South China Sea coastline in Fujian Province.

Xiamen Airlines operate three Boeing 737-200s and four Boeing 737-500s for their inter-provincial routes. Boeing 737-200 *B-2516* waits for clearance after pushback at Beijing Capital airport to operate a flight to Nanjing and on to Xiamen in June 1993.

(Left)
The four Boeing 757s of Xiamen Airlines have taken over many of the high-density routes previously operated by the Boeing 737s. *B-2828* creeps through the early morning mist on Guangzhou's taxiway in preparation to operate MF8306 to Xiamen.

(Below)
B-2828 on a more recent occasion arrives at Hong Kong operating its new daily flight from mainland Xiamen.

Wuhan Airlines

In 1988, the Municipal Government of the City of Wuhan formed Wuhan Airlines, also known as Air Wuhan. The airline commenced operations with two Yunshuji Y-5s and four Ilyushin Il-14s from Wuhan–Hankou airport on the north-west bank of the Yangtse River. As the airline expanded four Yunshuji Y-7s were added to the fleet, followed by three Boeing 737-300s. The acquisition of the Boeing 737s forced Wuhan Airlines to move across the river to the south-west corner of the city where the more modern airport of Wuhan–Wang Jia Dun is situated.

Four Czechoslovakian-built Avia 14 piston-engined airliners were initially purchased from the Air Force. The four examples lasted three years until they were retired in favour of the Y-7. *B-4211* awaits patronage at Wuhan–Hankou on a sunny day in November 1988.

(Above)
B-2918 prepares to depart from Guangzhou after operating the airline's inaugural Boeing 737 flight.

(Left)
Four Yunshuji Y-7-100 with winglets were selected to replace the ageing Avia 14s of Wuhan Airlines. The compact little fifty-two-seat turboprop airliners operate the local and short haul inter-provincial routes from Wuhan. *B-3442* is almost ready to depart from Beijing to Wuhan in October 1990.

Sichuan Airlines

In 1986, Sichuan Airlines was formed as a provincial airline of Sichuan Province financed by the Sichuan Government. The airline's first flight took place two years later in July 1988, when a Yunshuji Y-7 flew from Chengdu to Wanxian, situated along the banks of the famous Yangtse River. Sichuan Airlines used two CAAC turboprop Y-7s for their local routes until 1990 when the airline added two more Y-7s to the fleet. 1990 was also the year the airline adopted their new colours and identity. Late in 1991, the first Tu-154M arrived to take up its new position with the airline and during January 1992 the Tu-154M operated its maiden flight for Sichuan Airlines from Chengdu to Beijing. The airline continued its overall expansion from its base at Chengdu-Shuangliu Airport and into 1995 Sichuan Airlines now operate five Yunshuji Y-7s on local and inter-regional routes, whilst the five Tu-154Ms operate the longer inter-provincial routes serving twenty-one Chinese cities. Seven routes are served within Sichuan Province and another thirty-six routes are served nationwide.

Sichuan Airlines Tu-154M *B-2626* leaves
Beijing Capital airport on a flight destined
for Chengdu in June 1993.

The five Yunshuji Y-7 airliners provide local and short haul inter-provincial services from their Chengdu base to Changsha, Chongqing, Guilin, Guiyang, Luzhou, Nanchong, Wanxian, Wuhan, Xichang and Yibin. *B-3497* fresh from overhaul and a re-paint waits to rejoin the fleet on a typically dark cloudy day at Chengdu in March 1995

Yunnan Airlines (3Q)

Yunnan Airlines, formerly part of the CAAC Yunnan Regional Authority, was established as the provincial airline of the Province in 1992 from its base at Kunming–Wu Jiabao airport. Seven Boeing 737-300s are operated daily to Beijing, Shanghai and Guangzhou, and non-daily to twenty-two other Chinese cities. Internationally, the Boeing 737s operate the tourist routes from Kunming to Bangkok and Singapore.

Yunnan Airlines Boeing 737-300 *B-2539* waits to depart from Guangzhou in November 1993.

Great Wall Airlines (GW)

During 1994, the CAAC Flying College at Guanghan in Sichuan Province formed its own passenger airline under the control of CAAC and known as Air Great Wall. The airline flies two leased Aeroflot Tu-154Ms in Air Great Wall colours. From its base at Chongqing-Jiangbei airport the two Tu-154Ms operate to Beijing, Guangzhou, Haikou, Shanghai, Shenzhen and Wenzhou. During April 1995, Great Wall Airlines took delivery of the three remaining Air China Boeing 737-200s.

Inbound from Chongqing, *B-2628* makes a fine sight as it approaches Guangzhou for landing in November 1993.

Shenzhen Airlines

Shenzhen Airlines was established in January 1993 as a municipal joint venture airline. The principal administrators are CAAC and the Shenzhen Government with financial investment from Air China, Overseas Chinese City Economic Development Corporation, Bank of China and Shenzhen South Tongfa Industrial Corporation. Whilst the airline was being established the new Shenzhen-Huangtian Airport was being completed and during September 1993 both airport and airline became operational with a new Boeing 737-300 performing the inaugural scheduled flight from the new airport to Beijing. Shenzhen Airlines now operate to Beijing, Shanghai, Nanjing, Jinan, Zhengzhou, Chengdu, Wuhan, Haikou, Wenzhou, Meixian, Guiyang, Xiamen, Kunming, Ningbo, Hanzhou, Huangyan, Huangshan, Sanja, Changsha and Changzhou. Currently four Boeing 737-300s carry the Shenzhen Airline colours and by 1997 is expected to increase the fleet to ten Boeing 737-300s.

The second Boeing 737-300 of Shenzhen Airlines awaits delivery to the airline in August 1993.

Hainan Airlines

Plans were laid down in 1989 to establish the provincial airline of Hainan Island. The task was achieved under a joint ownership between the Hainan Government and CAAC. It took until April 1993 before the first of four Boeing 737-300s were available and ready to commence services from the sub-tropical holiday destination of Hainan Island situated in the China Sea. Also in April 1993 the company released a staff share float that enabled its workers to buy into the airline. From the island's capital airport of Haikou, Hainan Airlines has grown steadily and operates to Beijing, Guangzhou, Chongqing, Zhengzhou, Jinan, Shenzhen, Nanjing, Shanghai, Qingdao, Wenzhou, Nanchang, Wuhan, Changsha and Guiyang. The airline is in advanced planning stages to open new routes from the island to Hong Kong, Taiwan and other local Asian countries.

B-2578 is ready to leave Gate 3 at Xian-Xianyang Airport operating flight H4168 back to Haikou.

Guizhou Airlines

Guizhou Airlines, a small provincial airline flying from Guiyang, was founded by the Guizhou Government in 1993 to operate local air services in the southern half of China. The airline operates one seventeen-seater Yunshuji Y-12 and two fifty-two-seater Yunshuji Y-7s to nine local inter-provincial destinations in mountainous terrain.

Zhongyuan Airlines

Zhongyuan Airlines was established in 1991 as the provincial airline of Henan Province. From its capital and base airport of Zhengzhou the airline started with two Yunshuji Y-7s serving fifteen destinations within China. In April 1994 the airline took delivery of its first Boeing 737-300 in order to overcome the propeller ban in place at several Chinese airports.

(Left)
Air Guizhou Y-7-100 swoops into Guangzhou operating a charter flight during November 1993.

(Above)
Zhongyuan Airlines Yunshuji Y-7-100 with winglets *B-3439* prepares to depart from Beijing Capital airport in June 1993.

Shaanxi Airlines

Shaanxi Airlines is the oldest of the provincial airlines. The airline operated three vintage Ilyushin Il-14 airliners on tourist charters and general aviation duties from its base at Taiyuan-Wusu airport. The airline suspended all flying after an accident at Linfen in 1988. The company remained intact until the early part of 1995 when three Yunshuji Y-7s were delivered for resumption of local and inter-provincial air services.

The last of a generation of early piston-engined airliners awaiting its fate. *B-4217*, withdrawn from use for five years when this picture was taken in November 1993 at Taiyuan-Wusu airport.

Air Changan Airlines

During 1991, ACA–Air Changan Airlines was formed as a small municipal airline under a joint venture agreement with the Shaanxi Government, Shaanxi Aircraft Company and Xian Aircraft Company, the latter two being the local manufacturers of the Yunshuji Y-7. Two Y-7-100s operate a small route network from the airline's base at Xian-Xianyang Airport to Datong, Wuhan, Yinchuan and Yulin. Both the airline's Y-7-100s are painted in their attractive red colours and recently a third aircraft has been added to the fleet from China Eastern Airlines.

B-3707 awaits its patrons at Xian-Xianyang Airport in March 1995 for flight AG405 to Chongqing. The round trip takes four hours flying over some inhospitable wild mountain ranges; the area is the natural home of the Chinese Panda bears.

CAAC Flying College

The CAAC Flying College was re-organised frm the CAAC Air Training Division in 1986 and based at Guanghan in Sichuan Province. The college started with three Yunshuji Y-7-100s as pilot trainers and in 1990 took delivery of four Piper PA-42 Cheyenne six-seater turboprop aircraft for advanced training. The college still retains its three Y-7-100s but has increased its Cheyennes to six.

Piper Cheyenne, *B-3623* is seen at Xian-Xianyang Airport during a rare visit on an unscheduled refuelling stop in March 1995.

Chinese Aviation Industry

The Chinese aircraft manufacturing industry has been active ever since its first aircraft, a Feng Ru-2 biplane (similar to the Wright brothers' machine), flew in 1909.

Many types of Russian-designed military aircraft have been mass-produced under licence in China using a Chinese type name. All of the early MiG fighters, Yak trainers and Ilyushin bombers and even some Mil helicopters have been born on China's aviation production lines. The civil aircraft production has not been as active as the military production.

The Yunshuji Y-5 biplane is, of course, a licence-built Antonov An-2. Two production lines were established at Nanchang and Shijiazhuang. Both lines produced a total of approximately five hundred aircraft when the line closed in 1990. The Yunshuji Y-7 airliner, similar to the Antonov An-24, is manufactured at Yanliang in the Hanzhong District of Xian. Just over seventy of the airliners have been constructed at the rate of ten per year and delivered to seventeen Chinese airlines and two airlines outside China. Heavy maintenance was also undertaken at Yanliang for the Y-7, however, when the Chengdu maintenance factory 103 was closed to Ilyushin Il-14s and Il-18s it was converted exclusively for the maintenance of the Y-7s and An-24s.

During March 1995, we, the authors of *Chinese Airlines* visited the factory airfield at Yanliang and were regrettably denied photographic coverage, however, we are able to report extensive progress with China's only airliner. The Y-7-200A, of which three examples were present, is a Y-7 without winglets, has a fish-eye window just behind the cockpit like an An-26 and is fitted with five-bladed curved propellers. The Y-7-500 is in initial production as the all cargo version of the Y-7, having winglets, a fish-eye window behind the cockpit, four-bladed straight propellers and a rear loading cargo ramp exactly the same as the An-26, four examples were present including the prototype. Note: Also at Yanliang was the production line for the vintage Tu-16 bomber being manufactured for the Chinese Air Force, fourteen examples were present. In another large building in full production was the tails, rudders and flaps for the Boeing 737s and wing section for the ATR-42.

The Yunshuji Y-8, similar to the An-12, appears to have ceased production at Yanliang.

Sometime around 1970, Shanghai Aviation Industrial Corporation designed a one-hundred-and-seventy-eight-seat, four-engined jet airliner similar in shape to the Boeing 707 and designated the 'Shanghai Yunshuji Y-10'. The first prototype was used at Xian in the late 1970s for static testing. The second prototype took to the air on its maiden flight in September 1980. Test flights on CAAC routes were undertaken from Shanghai to Harbin and Urumqi until 1984. Between 1985 and 1986 the second prototype was parked at Beijing Capital airport out of commission, and by 1987 this valuable prototype had been moved elsewhere. Regrettably its fate is unknown.

Harbin Aircraft Industries at Pingfang produced the Y-11 piston-engined, multi-purpose aircraft between 1975 and 1983. Production ceased in favour of the Y-12 turboprop version. Since 1983, it is believed that approximately forty examples have been built and sold.

An early example of Chinese-built airliners was the 'Beijing 1' prototype. Only one example was developed and constructed in 1958 by the Beijing Aeronautical Institute as a passenger-carrying airliner. This valuable example is displayed in a large courtyard at the Beijing Aeronautical Institute in the southern Beijing suburbs.

(Right)
B-548L, although not a Y-12 prototype, is an early example used by the Pingfang factory as a demonstration aircraft bearing CAAC titles in an attractive red colour.

(Below)
Line-up of Y-11s and Y-12s at the test airfield at Pingfang, Heilongjiang Province.